THE SAM
BACK

FRANK DULLAGHAN

Published by Cinnamon Press
Meirion House,
Glan yr afon,
Tanygrisiau
Blaenau Ffestiniog,
Gwynedd, LL41 3SU
www.cinnamonpress.com

ISBN: 978-1-909077-40-9
British Library Cataloguing in Publication Data. A CIP record for this book can be obtained from the British Library.

Designed and typeset in Palatino by Cinnamon Press
Cover from original artwork 'slow implosion' by Aidan Dullaghan © Aidan Dullaghan
Cover design by Jan Fortune Printed in Poland
Cinnamon Press is represented in the UK by Inpress Ltd www.inpressbooks.co.uk and in Wales by the Welsh Books Council www.cllc.org.uk

Acknowledgements

A number of these poems, sections of them, or earlier versions of them, were published in the following journals: *All Roads Will Lead You Home* (vacpoetry.org USA); *Causeways* (Ireland) *Cyphers* (Ireland); *Irish Literary Review* (Ireland); *The Journal* (UK); *Lampeter Review* (UK); *Magma* (UK); *The Moth* (Ireland); *New Contrast* (South Africa); *PN Review* (UK); *The Poetry Bus* (Ireland); *Poetry Review* (UK); *Reactions 3* (UK); *Riptide Journal* (UK); *The Shop* (Ireland); *Smiths Knoll* (UK); *Sukoon* (Dubai)

The following anthology publications are acknowledged: *Nowhere Near a Damn Rainbow – Unsanctioned Writing from the Middle East* – The Poeticians – Xanadu Press (Lebanon) 2012 – Edited: Hind Shoufani (*One Minute You're Lost*); *Newspaper Taxis* –

Poetry After the Beatles – Seren 2013 – Edited: Phil Bowen, Damian Furniss and David Woolley (*Back in the USSR*); *Poets Quest for God* – Eyewear Publishing 2014 – Edited: Todd Swift (*Even in the Midst of Grief*); *From the City to the Saltings* – Essex Poetry Festival Anthology 2014 (*Winter Fields*)

A version of *Pay Attention* was commended in the *Sentinel Literary Quarterly* Competition 2012 and published in that journal. *My Mother Walking*, was published in the Dubai Irish Society's 2014 Annual.

I'd like to thank Danna, my wife Marie, Rewa and Zeina with whom I've work-shopped many of these poems. As always, a big thank you goes to my son Aidan for the wonderful cover artwork. A special thanks is due to Zeina Hachem Beck for providing a platform, *Punch*, where some of these poems were first performed and, in particular, for her close reading of most of the poems. Likewise, thank you to Hind Shoufani for the *Poeticians* platform. Finally, as previously, thanks are also due to Ann Drysdale for her close reading and assistance in structuring the final manuscript.

Frank Dullaghan lives in Dubai. He holds an MA with Distinction in Writing from the University of South Wales. Whilst in the UK he co-founded the *Essex Poetry Festival* and edited *Seam Poetry Magazine* He has two previous poetry collections (*On the Back of the Wind*, 2008, and *Enough Light to See the Dark*, 2012) from Cinnamon Press. He has also published two haiku collections. Frank is a poetry judge for the Emirates Airline Festival of Literature where in 2015, for a second time, he will be reading on an international platform. His screenplay *Melody* featured in the best short films Dubai 48 hour Film competition 2012 and won the audience award in the Mumbai Women's International Film Festival 2013. He regularly reads with the *Poeticians* and *Punch* spoken word collectives. His short stage plays, *Crossing the Road* and *DNA*, featured at the Short & Sweet Festival 2013 and 2014 respectively. He has also had other short scripts performed or screened. He is currently working on a number of writing projects including a short documentary film script, a feature length screenplay and a novel. He is a regular book reviewer for the Dubai Eye *Talking of Books* radio programme.

Contents

For my brothers and sisters:
John, Tommy, Mary and Rosemarie
May you always find your own roads back

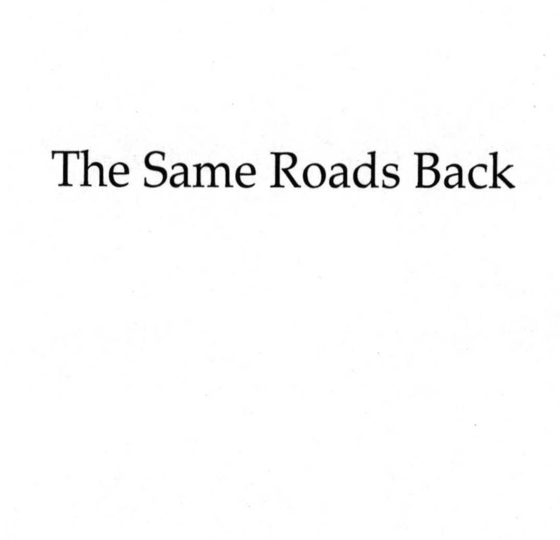

The Same Roads Back

The Street of Lost Gloves

The first one I noticed seemed to be crawling off the pavement,
one finger darker than the rest, where the tip touched
the gutter puddle, as if it were trying to make its way home,
one finger slightly raised, in the act perhaps, of hailing a taxi,

or falling back in the disappointment of having missed one.
On a window ledge, a red mitten, flat on its back,
too long in the sun. In against the wall of a house,
a dark brown leather one with its fingers curled,

its glassy gold fastening stud like an eye, questioning.
And the others – wool, leather, cotton, silk, all colours, all sizes,
on the pavement, in doorways, and one small pink one
trapped under the wheel of a chained bicycle.

What gathered them here? It doesn't seem a popular route
from anywhere to anywhere else. But maybe
this is where the lost end up, in this nowhere street,
emptying their hands of the one glove left to them.

A Way with Words

My earliest memory is of conversation,
my mother standing by the gate and talking
to a neighbour. I was astonished
by its give and take, wondered how
one went about it. I was maybe
two years old, the wrought-iron gate
higher than my head. I looked through
its bars at our neighbour's little girl and
said something. She was evidently as enveloped
in this great happening as I and
gave me back a tiny tumble of words.
And so we pitched and caught
small handfuls of what we knew
without much sense or continuity
until we quickly ran out of things to say
and stood defeated, our mothers still
going strong. I remember a wave
of such disappointment and then a high regard
for my mother who had a bucketful of words
and could tip them out all day.

Snow Falling After Dark

It was too late to be young
when she cycled home from that day's work
to a house gone dark with illness:
her mother and father, neither knowing
that the other was dying.

She stayed at home, tended them,
one upstairs, one down.
Her brothers came in for their meals,
crowded the table with noise.

She had no time to remember the few boys
she had kissed. *Daddy*, she'd say lifting
the weight of that name in the bed.
She was not recognised by her mother
who'd gone decades young in her head.

But still she got up to the sound
of the milk cart in the street, put breakfast out
and tried to forget the hands
that she'd held at the dances
when her life was a road over hills,
not curtained small into rooms.
They died within days of each other.

There was nothing frivolous about the man
that she found, six years older than herself,
as lost to the world as she was,
but love arrived like snow falling after dark
so that the days they entered
were bright and clean, a beginning.

Kneeling

Our garden grass was long enough
for wind to sculpt it every day,
for dock and dandelion to flourish, frogs
to gather up an army in its dark.

Each year before the blessing of the graves
drew walkers past our waist-high
garden wall, my mother would kneel
on a piece of carpet and clip all that grew

to within an inch of its roots.
She worked the shears for hours, three days
in a row. Its bad haircut was clumped
and yellow-stalked, unlike the green perm

tightness of our neighbours' lawns,
the uneven under-surface showing through
in dip and rise. Yet it was clean.
More than this, it showed a neighbourly

act of labour that was enough
not to *let the terrace down*.
I would smell the green sap on her hands
like something wild, unlike her other smells

of baked bread and ironed clothes,
and grew excited by this difference
until I was old enough to take her place,
kneeling in a green state of grace.

My Mother Walking

My mother matched the two halves
of a £200 pound note,
hunted out of packets of Daz
(prayed for, found) and so
walked with me the mile road into town
to that shop that still served us
through my father's unemployment;
walked past the red-brick terraces
with their doors opened (their hallways
like the long tongues of dogs) onto the hot street,
walked for the first time in years
that same road that I walked home each week
with butter and spuds, sugar and scallions, whatever
was on the short list she wrote out
for the manager who quietly wrote-off our debt.
I would watch the weals from the brown leather straps
of the grocery bag raise up on my arms
when I stopped to rest. When she stepped
into his shop, he told her she looked well,
gave her a seat in his small office, a cup of sweet tea
and the change from her cashed cheque.
He placed a bar of butterscotch into my hand
when we stood up to go, my other hand in the hand
of my mother for the short walk home.

My Mother's Blond-haired Boy

My mother showed me once –
an off-white envelope, maybe buff, and
inside, a small lock of hair. Mine.

For my first two years, I was
a blond blue-eyed boy.
Then I turned dark.

I remember the soft curl of it:
something
I could no longer return to.

I may have been seven or eight
when she showed me,
but still that loss, that sudden insight

into Time's relentless rush,
of being unable to replace
the version of myself

that hit the high note,
that filled-in all the boxes, for her.
It was like we shared

the heartbreak of it – that short time
when her world was perfect
and I shone in it like the sun.

That Summer of Grass

I remember the loaf of the back door step,
hot in that summer of grass, the grass
high as my head; the way I broke through it,
making my own maze, a place to lie back.

My mother would sing my return,
until my weekend father came home
from his week-away job and the language
of the house changed. Rooms became untidy,
meals struggled to meet appetite, the unsaid
hung heavy in each room. Windows were closed.

And I wondered, why he could not stay away,
leave me to sail into the sky from the green sea
of the garden, leave me with my mother
raising her white sail of sheets to the sun.

My Mother Flew Off and Left Us

She first felt the grip on her heart
as she waited for the excursion bus to Lourdes.
Her companions were too full of their approaching journey
to notice. She held her breath
carefully, like borrowed money.

But she came back from Lourdes time-marked,
finding the weight of her life hard to lift,
feeling the flutter
of what was to come perched in her chest.

Later, home from hospital, she flew.
She shrugging off her body like an old coat,
lifted free into mid-morning air, leaving it all –
the flat-roofed coal house, the uncombed garden,
her boys seated in a classroom's windowed shaft of dust,
her husband off at work in Dublin
not knowing he had started to fall or how hard
he'd yet to hit the ground.

She Dreams of Fat Babies

For Zeina

She awakes from dreams of fat babies
to the rush of the school run, the new pang
of parting from her youngest, the tiny triumph of time
to read, write, enjoy the drawl of a mall coffee.
But now she's more aware of what seems
like a parade of newborn, their shine of life startling
the morning, shoppers melting around prams, and
she can't stop thinking about those babies –

the loll of their small heads when lifted, their warm
weight, their smell. Everywhere she goes she notices
the easy mothers, still tummied and tired
but with those soft prizes parceled in their arms
to be peered at, to astonish: their dark eyes drinking
all of it in, their perfect fingers and thumbs.

Freezing Fog

As I move, the space about me
re-shapes itself:
buildings resolving into solidity,
quiet people moving into and out of focus.
Nothing is certain or fixed.
Only the map in my head keeps me straight.
I feel old. Mid-morning. February.
I'm starting on a three-hour journey to a late shift.
My tall son is already at college.
He will be trying to follow patterns,
trying to focus as his mind whitens.
Yesterday he stared at the wall –
two hours unplugged from the world.
His doctor says he needs structure,
that the drugs will kick in in a few weeks.
For now, what's real keeps unpeeling.
He sleeps a lot. Outside my carriage window
the landscape lengthens, the sky lifts.
Two Indian boys sit next to me.
I listen to the music of their talk.
It seems a long time before I realise
they are speaking in English.

Blanket

Now that he's normal again, he forgets
that the summer turning brown
and that edge of ice in the breath of morning
means that college term begins
and he must begin
repeating his disrupted year, must face

new faces and wait for them
to think him odd, wandering up the field
at lunchtime to eat his sandwiches alone,
where the only close sound
is the sound of the grass kissing the breeze
there and there and there, and where

his mind can follow its own tune
and settle into the comfort of that rhythm,
not think about the instructions
the art teacher gave for his *Journeys* project
or how she couldn't see
that this had to be about a mad scientist

taking control of every mind by pointing
his insane machine and how the only safe place
to think this through is the field
where the earth can rise around you
like a blanket of love
that shuts out the glare of the world.

She Forgot to Put Time On

She forgot to put time on that morning
and walked out under the sky
without its caution, its keeping.

The clouds were busy at their easels,
the sun on its throne.

It was a day when love seemed possible,
the breeze brushing against her face,
traffic conversing with itself.

It was a day when the body
could forget and skip
out of its stricture of silence.

So she answered the man who spoke to her
as they stepped off the train
they had taken into the city.

He smiled at her
and she wrapped that smile like a gift

and except that time had a grip on his wrist,
he would, she is sure, have wanted
to ask her to go somewhere for a coffee.

So she went by herself
and sat with a latte and a strawberry cake

and forgot about work, the need
to arrive, the time it might take.

Looking at the World

Home was an end-of-terrace
on the road running out of town,
its white pebble-dash bright
till the years grimed it dull. My father
was a great critic of our neighbours'
ungodliness, the whole of the terrace and
beyond in the grip of sin. He could see it
in their lust for good jobs, their motor cars,
the way they'd gone beyond themselves
building garages out the back, eating
in restaurants, like swanks, above in the town.

In the other direction, the road snuck away
to the border and on into the North, a land
stolen by Protestants, sinners who were
ten times worse than our neighbours,
not much better, I was let know, than pagans
and destined to join that great multitude
of our own, as I pictured it, crowding for entry
around the gates of hell. The North for me
was a place of imagination;
a country lost in the shadows of history,
in the news of bombings and killings;
a country where only those with cars ventured.
Being pedestrian, my father kept to the small roads
of our own parish, the easy ways home.

Years later in London, I met a girl who'd spent
her childhood growing up amongst Puerto Ricans.
She was twelve before she saw her first
blue-eyed boy and was shocked, she told me,
by the thought of how cold the world must look
from behind those eyes. I felt then that I knew
the truth of that. For whether the world is cold
or is browned by a warm sun is in the eyes
of the beholder, and I could see then
that my father always looked out at the world
with his eyes cast down.

Captain of the Debating Team

The Dundalk schools debating competition. The De La Salles –
a poor boy's school. No Blazers, no badges, no previous
history of competing. Sure losers. Good for a laugh. We were
in it because our English teacher was young, was new.
Dullaghan, he said, *I'm counting on you. I think you might
have the cheek to win,* and made me captain. I think it was
because I had the longest hair in the school. *Rebel,* he thought.
Jesus, I thought, but took the whole thing very seriously.

The St. Louise Convent Girls were our first opponents.
Immaculate. Boarding school money. Previous runners-up
looking for salvation. *It's a man's world,* the topic. *Watch them,*
the teacher told me, *they're not as sweet as they look.
Nor the nuns as holy. They'll play dirty*. He handed me a book –
The Second Sex by Simone de Beauvoir, a 1940's book
banned in holy Ireland. *Don't let your father see you with this.
The girls will have read it*. 1971 trying to break out

of the 50's. The girls opened with artificial insemination.
The audience was shocked; virgin flesh so knowing.
I asked if this required injection, if one prick was as good
as another. A cheap joke but showed I'd engaged, that their
use of the word *penis* would not stutter me. I complemented
the girls on their looks. They smiled, preened. I noted it.
I was merciless, sexist. I finished a quotation from de Beauvoir
begun by the girl's captain, summing up. I had expected it.

This book is necessary reading, I held the banned volume up.
Until it's understood, it will always be a man's world. We won.
The Christian Brothers boys were something else. The finals.
Previous winners. Bright. At the end, the judges thought them
learned in debate. They thought us *smart*. I was singled out
for the way I'd worked the audience. *Applause and twist
of tongue do not win the argument*. It was a sort of upper class
moment in a working class town. Upstarts back in place. But

they'd had a taste of us. Their world no longer safe.
Afterwards my teacher handed me an under-age dark pint.
Don't tell your father. And that was something too.

Border Boy

Being a border boy, I knew those small lanes between holdings,
the boreens that bypassed the border checkpoints.
I was fifteen or so, learning to fly by myself. I understood that

a subsidy on exported butter and high VAT rendered that butter
cheaper in the British-governed north, five miles from home.
I became an immediate entrepreneur, what my fellow countrymen

would have called *"cute"*. Circumstances will sometimes
arrange themselves for success. I solicited orders, collected money,
got on my bike with an empty box. It was all uphill going north,

downhill home (I told you circumstances conspired). Back on my
side of the border, forty pounds of yellow Irish butter later,
I stopped on the crest of the last hill, looked down through the dark

to the lit road of my own terrace, the sky soft as a poached salmon
behind the houses. I pushed off, free-wheeling home.
I was half-way down when a shadow entered the road, a loud voice

in a *Gardā* uniform. Had I swerved, he'd have hauled me down.
I yelled that I had no brakes and headed towards his opening arms,
an arrow to a target; a lover to a dark embrace, then watched

his last minute leap aside, heard the splash as he landed wet;
his bellow at my back *I know you McNulty*. My wings opened
at his error and my heart soared over the terrace, free.

The Coal Bucket

Galvanised metal, it clanged on the floor
of the coalhouse and again as I shoveled
coal into it. Those black rocks gleamed grudgingly
under the light and I could smell its dust
in the air. I'd lug it into the yard, bouncing it
off my shin when I wasn't careful,
my hands filthy when I'd haul it in to stand
against the wall near the inset range.

On winter mornings my mother got up early,
had the kitchen heated before I came down,
my hair more awake than myself, my bedraggled
schoolbag and uncertain homework
dropped in the hall. When someone announced
that the old man up the terrace had
kicked the bucket, I wondered if it had been
empty or full at the time; if he'd stubbed
his toes clanging into it, or tipped it over,
spilling coal and slack on his kitchen floor,
and if he'd rubbed his hands on his trousers
to clean them, like he was not supposed to.

Back in the USSR

for Fergus

I was born in Ireland too late
for Beatle mania. Yet they opened a door
in our town and the small desires of the Fifties –
formica kitchens, labour saving appliances –
went out while less easy ones stepped in. Freedom
was the word we used for this but never understood.
The big girl next door said the Beatles were the thing
and so they were. We learned the words and sung
the tunes like anthems of a revolution
against domestic obedience, an expectant Church.
We talked excitedly of *Hari Krishna* and LSD, and although
a long way from the daily pain of Vietnam, we wanted
Peace to have its chance. It was a sort of education.
I stacked shelves in *Dunne's Stores* to buy *Sgt Pepper*
clothes. My elder brother listened to them
on his new transistor radio, the same one
on which he heard, he said, real-time
Radio Free Prague crashed into silence. He said
he heard the jackboots on the stairs, the studio door
bashed in. He became a local celebrity of sorts,
an authority on East European politics, for a while.
But everything goes back to those who fuck
the rest, those with wealth and power or who
have stepped up to the plate and grabbed a handful.
Yet these words of Freedom, Love and Peace
are like a fever. The virus lives on, there's been
an unexpected outbreak in the *Arab Spring*.
I listen to my son who's strumming *Back to the USSR*
on his guitar, as if there's no redemption in the past,
as if everything that's won is somehow lost.

Tasting the Air

In the park he bounded at the air,
straining against the leash, the wide space
pulling him. Years kept in a back yard
till this: the boyfriend of a daughter
of the house feeling sorry for him.
Don't let him off the leash, I was told,
he's attacked children, scared them.
I could see that he would, thuggish
black nightmare with a grinful of teeth.

For the world to be right, a dog,
imprisoned for so long, needed to run.
So I ran with him, the leash lashed
to my wrist. Young, fit, I sprinted
the green, he in full stride beside me.
I sprinted until his lungs gave out,
until I was pulling at heaviness,
at a gasping weight of dog flesh.
And so we sat on the grass, he and I,
letting our tongues taste the moving air.

The Fridge Inside Her

The fridge inside her wants her to hoard cheese,
it wants her to play it cool. It whispers of ice, the need
to keep raw meat fresh, to open up brightly

to anyone who approaches looking hungry.
The fridge inside her purrs, it wants her to sit quietly,
be receptive, a keeper of plums and tomatoes,

a place where vegetables can shrivel slowly,
where microwaveable meals can congregate,
their little yellow saver stickers curling at the edges.

The fridge inside her says she must keep everything
on its own shelf – heart on one, brain on another.
It says love should be frozen if she wants to make it last.

Turning

I didn't think much about it at the time
not knowing it was the last.
Now I'm walking backwards
my coat tightening in from its swirl,
knowing just how to turn without colliding,
and there at the edge of my eye,
as I turn back through street, wall, railing,
is the lift of your hair,
threading what's left of the sun
through the air, spilling in on itself,
composing itself on your shoulders
as you step backwards too,
and turn,
your face rising from its shadow
and mine opening into a smile
as if nothing had happened,
as if everything had stayed the same.

A Man Falling

A man is falling.
The building blurs,
windows wiped
of his reflection
in an instant. He
looks small as a doll
but I cannot save him.
If my watching
eyes could wish,
they would wash him
out of the air; they
would have him back,
ten floors up,
behind the rail
of his balcony.
What is he thinking?
Is he calling out or is
that just the boom
of my own blood?

A man is falling,
the pavement slowly
climbing towards his
speeding brain,
each grain of air lost
to him in passing.
As he dips under
the street lamp, his
shadow leaps from him,
its open arms ready
to receive him, a
last embrace, a final
journey into himself.

Now there are police,
an ambulance,
a small crowds of people.
But I don't go over.
The only way
I can save him
is to hold him
forever in the air.

How the Artist Passed His Interview

For Aidan

It was clear that everyone else had heavy portfolios
of work with them. The edges of oils and acrylics
blazed their colours underarm or from leather carriers.
He had a few items in his rucksack, pencil-
on-paper sketches, some biro line drawings.

When they asked to see his work, he refused,
saying he wished to talk about it first. He told them
that as an artist he felt a need to go back to basics –
a white page, a pencil or pen. Even, he explained,

to the consideration of how to place a mark
on clean white paper. Because these are all things
that need to be thought about, experimented with.
The talking became a debate, a discussion.

When he showed them his work, they all crowded
around, looked closely, paid attention. He took out
a roll of wallpaper border, stooped to stand on one end,
then he unrolled it high above his head. On the back

in biro, he had drawn a ladder – two parallel vertical lines
with horizontal crossings. Simple. Basic. He called it
Do you believe in the Lord God Almighty?
They called it *Art*.

How the Artist Became an Artist

For Aidan

It was the time for his final installation and
nothing would work. His allocated space
against a wall with a window was poor, did not
fit his need to have the audience interact with his art.

All of his efforts and ideas failed. *It's rubbish,*
he thought. The whole year had been the same:
running to catch a bus that wouldn't stop and
which was going in the wrong direction anyway.

When the examination board came to view his work
they found one of the institutes large metal dustbins,
the art torn and broken, though arranged within and
around the bin. They determined that an explanation

was required before they could mark it. *It's rubbish,*
he told them. *Everything I did this year is rubbish. This
is the only way to display it appropriately*. They were
taken with his artistic response and marked it high.

When it came time for the public viewing,
to their dismay, the bin and contents had been removed
overnight by the cleaners. They approached the artist.
Don't worry, he told them, *the only thing to do*

with rubbish, is to throw it out. They were awestruck.
The actualisation of the artistic concept, they said
to each other and felt vindicated in their high marking,
knew they were in the presence of a true artist.

Clean Poem

You asked me to write a clean poem
so I write about soap, where it can take you

when you undress it from its wrap;
the hard smooth feel of it in your hand.

It can take you into your bath.
Look how it travels the length of your arm,

moves down your belly, the slip
and slide of it, its long deep strokes.

Soon you are all of a lather. See
how it lifts you clean from the water,

your breath misting the mirror, the sheen
on your skin, that after-glow, that heat

of you wrapped into towels, the softness
that comes upon you now that it's done.

(I don't mean it like that! You should
wash out your mouth!) This is a story,

the story of soap. Yes, just as you asked,
this is a clean poem. Read it over.

Dirty Poem

You asked me to write you a dirty poem,
the kind that might get under your fingernails,

cause you to toss and turn in bed,
the sheets twisting like ropes, constricting.

Maybe you are blindfolded, gagged.
Perhaps you like a certain level of pain –

the kind that bleeds from your TV news:
real enough to smart but not to hurt; to jolt

the dinner conversation but not the appetite.
You know what I'm talking about. It's all

about role-play, levels of participation.
There are safe words you can use

like *house, afternoon-tea, shopping*.
This is not something that you indulge in

often. There are children with dead eyes
in the garden, women gone beyond grief.

There are men growing into wolves,
picking at their teeth. There are bombs.

There is darkness where homes sat warm.
There is pain by the ton. You can have

your ounce. Raise your ass just a little
higher for me, Dear. See, I told you

this is a dirty poem. It's all in the head.

Blue

i.m. Dara Delargey

Dead: no longer in the world.
That's hard to drink down.

Suppose the colour *blue* stopped
being refracted, was taken

from the spectrum. Sky and sea
would never look the same.

You might hold that colour
in your head for as long as you could

(there's comfort in that, certainly)
but it isn't the thing itself.

Woods in summer would lose
their magic. Some eyes might

turn transparent. How can you
measure such a loss? You can't.

Not at the time. It's afterwards,
when you look back at the world, see

everything in it that has been changed.
That's when you'll know,

that's when you can count it all up.
Father, please take this cup....

Even in the Midst of Grief

For Bernie

Even in the midst of grief the hands break
bread, the mouth eats. Even in grief,
the body has its small circle of comfort –
a cool bed, sun blessing the face.
The future continues to sail in
with its hold and its decks full.
Even in the midst of grief the body walks
the shore gathering stones;
gathering the wide sea into the heart.

Even when the heart thinks its life is over,
one could come who will change all
that has gone before. Just as each new wave
washes the previous one away.

She Puts on the Dark

She steps into her room and puts on the dark,
the house heavy-sighing. Outside, cold crisps
the air and she imagines his footsteps
as he crosses over the bridge, leaving, gone
like a leaf-boat launched into a river, a feather
taken up on the wind. He will never return.

This is what she is good at: scraping her own dinner
into the waste bin; seeing a new mirror cracked
at the moment of purchase. Life will never
hold her close, so she beats it to the punch,
stamping on her own sandcastle before another can.
There's satisfaction at least in giving no one else

that satisfaction. She excuses herself from the pain
of the world by merging with it so completely,
she becomes invisible. She becomes the dark and all
that it contains, as if she were born to it, relished it.
She puts on the dark and imagines his light growing
smaller and smaller, until it had never been.

Four Poems of the Arab Spring

i) Day of the Dogs
Syria 2012

The dogs are loose on the street,
they have loaded guns and they shoot.

They snarl, they bark, they bite. They would
gauge out your soul if they could.

See how they circle and strike,
pulling one from the crowd whom they kick

and beat bloody with the butt of a gun,
a pretty girl maybe, or one

whose smell they know and have sought
for some time to lay low. They ought

to be locked in their kennels but,
in these unusual times, they've been cut

from their leashes, sent out to savage and rend.
They rip softness from women, restraint from the men.

ii) One Minute You're Lost
Bahrain 2011

One minute you're lost in remembering
the complications of surgery, a young boy's chances,
(his eyes surprising you, green), the next
all thoughts crash to the wall where you're flung,
beaten to the ground. This is one of your country's
security forces personnel making the country safe.
(His slim, bony, legs, a flop of hair, childish freckles on pallid skin.)
You are pitched into a cell that smells of piss, of fear.

When they come for you, it's not what you expect.
The interrogation is a series of statements, no questions –
you did this, you did this.
Your back is raw, you have been introduced
to electricity. You think your heart stopped twice. (His lashes
were like a girls'.) Even when you say 'Yes, yes
I did.' they beat that answer deeper into you, as if they can
make you believe it, as if that will make it true.
The boy is long dead when they let you go.

iii) The Blue Spoon of the Sky
Syria 2012

Under the blue spoon of the sky the voice of a boy
is calling on his father to get up from the road.
Now the air explodes into noise. A tittle tattle
of bullet cases bounce onto your lap like the loss
of hope in the heart for a pause, for a way out.
And above, where blue has now fled behind smoke,
some god or other, yours or theirs (who cares?),
is laughing his broken laugh like a cough. It's enough
to wreck your mind. You are edging on mad.
Even the dogs have fled leaving you to your hate, to
your dead, to your day after day of killing, to the
smell of your own sweat, to this addiction you have
to the rolling dice of your life, where fear becomes
something forbidden you taste in your mouth
but keep coming back to like a tongue to the loss
of a tooth. Take your gun and go out. Take your chance
in your dance with death. Go on. Blow everything up.

iv) Their Bonfire-Brightened Nights
Egypt 2013

Those young men from their bonfire-brightened nights,
how can they sleep with so much changed for the worse?
They reach out with love but are ignored.
Their women and their children on the road
are hardly recognisable as themselves, they suffer
the blood-washed squares; their inner noise of grief;
the dead, who cannot leave these broken streets.

The dead who cannot leave these broken streets,
the blood-washed squares, their inner noise of grief,
are hardly recognisable as themselves. They suffer
their women and their children on the road.
They reach out with love but are ignored.
How can they sleep with so much changed for the worse:
those young men from their bonfire-brightened nights?

How We Survive

for Hind Shoufani

We have seen and heard so much
these past years: innocence woken too early
from its short sleep; grief
trying on so many new dresses.

Still the sky flies its yellow kite by day,
its white kite at night.
You need to be strong to step outside
the door of the heart.

And yet we do. This is how we progress,
pulling each day on like an old hat
we've grown used to,
letting our love roam,

an inquisitive child that won't be minded.
This is how we survive –
unbuttoning the coat of ourselves
to let our good friends close.

This May Be Your Moment

for Rewa Zeinati, who was in the moment

Time will always want more from you
than you have. It will own you
if you let it. It wants to hold your secrets
then give them away. Have no truck with it,
it measures out what it lets you spend
and what you can buy will be over too fast.

There is a certain glamour – the good
old days, a golden future. It would take you
by the wrist, pull you from the moment.
And the moment may be all that you have.
You might want to live in it, wear it
like a house or a country, a place maybe,

where you can forget. But time has no
patience, it waits for no one. It will lie,
it will say, *come in, I can heal you.*
It cannot. Healing is only in the moment.
You must give up time or it will drop you.
It will let you down at the end.

Songbird

for Zeina, Tripoli, Aug 2013

She opens the gate of her ribcage,
lets the bird of her heart fly out.
Away, she says, showing it the bitten moon,
the cut-out trees against the grey
blanket of sky. *Fly*, she tells it pointing
to the shivering sea, the hidden mountains
beyond. For what is there here for it
but the need to go blind, to lose its voice,
to break its back under the weight
of each day? Here they polish their pain
into currency. Here they trade in death. Here
they torture the small white body of the soul
until it gives up its ghost, leaving them
to their brutal flesh and bone, *Go*, she cries
to her heart, *and do not return. For they
would clip your wings, strangle your song.*

Naming the Stars

Syria 2013

I must learn to forgive the sun
its thirst for the dark:
it drinks the night down.

I would stay beneath night's cold
blanket. Not to be safe
but to be blind. Who wants to see

the body of a young girl on the street,
her eyes whitening; the wall
ripped from a neighbour's house

the wind reading his books,
spilling his memories onto the street;
faces of soldiers, a thousand years old,

who have stopped
counting their killings, who breathe
through their guns? Leave me the dark.

I will name the stars I can see
through the smoke, escapees, souls
who have been blown into the sky.

Leave me with all this death
as if it were a kind of love. Do not
let the sun see my face.

All Fall Down

All the birds fell like leaves.
Now they are heaped
in wind-fluffed mounds.

The sky fills with light
and we pretend
it is not empty, that
it's not edging away.

The land is filled
with bonfires.

Everything is going up
in smoke – feathers,
the words you will not say,
my anger, your hesitation.

I go down to the river
to watch the water move.

All of my memories stand
and look about.
They have nowhere to go.

But water has its own way
of listening.

I remember
how it seemed as if
the birds were clapping
as they fell.

Black & White

Café Supreme, Mall of the Emirates, 6th June 2013

They come in in their blacks,
two afterthoughts
behind the white grace of their husbands.

Only their eyes may be seen,
and their heels,
in the flap of their sandals.

One of the husbands is a boy,
still practising his beard.
The men wheel the baby buggies

which they park by the women
as the women flurry into chairs,
then they talk to each other,

man-to-man, and the women listen.
Then the women join in.
And this is allowed.

A waitress brings food.
One woman takes a baby onto her lap.
It nuzzles at her black.

One man spoon-feeds cake
to his older child.
The child watches

the father as if he were a riddle
that needed to be solved,
is careful opening its mouth.

The women's eyes are smiling,
their bodies tilted
towards their husbands.

The Heartache Café

For Hind Shufani

This is where the heartbroken come,
this low-ceilinged coffee house
with its dark aromas. You can see them
come through the door looking incomplete,
carrying what is absent like a wound.
See that girl, soft as a swan, she can no longer
open the wings of her life. See how
she taps at the table with the beak
of her fingers while her coffee grows cold.
That old man in the corner is made of glass.
He is cracked from the head to the heart.
If he moves he will shatter, glitter
across the floor like ice. The café
crouches around its hurt and will not
let them go. That boy has taken
two facing chairs. One of them will
always be empty. Now a woman comes
dragging her past, heaving it through the door.
She cannot open her hands and go free.
No one speaks. Some moan slowly
to themselves. Others shudder,
wet-faced, in their chairs. The waiter
keeps their cups full to the brim and is silent.
No one looks at the window where, outside,
sun may have lightened the day
or rain carry the scent of a mountain. No one
wants to let go of their pain.
They feel it is all that they have; to give it up
would be a betrayal. They have invested
so much of themselves in their aching
that they have no place else to be.
A dark-haired girl glimmers by the counter
as if making up her mind to go or stay, she holds
her coffee warm against her breast,
the light from the window
lifting shadows from her face.

Escalator

One step ahead of her,
going down the escalator,
he turns and rests his head
on her breasts,
as though this is normal,
as if this is a place
he would normally
rest his head
when the world
overwhelms him.
I pass him by, hurrying
down into the underground
to find my journey home
while he is already there,
his woman resting her hands
on the crown of his head.

Pay Attention

I will put our lake in a box.
It may make little quacking noises
but no one is paying attention.

I will lift the warmth of the sun
from the grass and stopper it
in a bottle. No one will heed
the sweat that beads on the glass.

Into this envelope, I will slot
the white disk of the moon.
Who will ever now see the dusting
of moth wings on its face?

The whole of the summer, I will
paste into this book. It may singe
its way through the spine but
there is no one to care;
no one is paying it any attention.

I will pack all of it away in the night
that sleeps under my bed and
I will set loose my memories of you
on the wind. No one will hear them pass.

The voice that you left in my head
will escape through the bars
of a shower, its notes washed bright.

And if it comes back to you,
you will think it only a bird, high
on some lonely branch
and will pay it no attention.

Chance

Like the sky falling
past the edge of the sea
(the sea shrugging itself
between shores,
light shared
between them).

Like snow
building itself up
on the stripped earth,
making everything bright
the way death
is supposed to.

Like the straight road
that leads on
but never out.
Like the arrow
awaiting its turn
in the quiver. Like love

and all of its shadows –
the glass placed down
at the end of a meal,
the lamp turned on
in the study.
Like everything

you would expect
and like nothing
at all.
Just itself
in its small place
in the turning universe.

Winter Field

(i)

The large black man sprawls in his chair.
He moves a lazy hand in answer
to the woman opposite him. Shoppers stroll by.
He lifts a small coffee cup to his lips.
I check my Blackberry again for word of funds.
My company is on a countdown to closure.

He leans back in his armchair and laughs softly,
his bulk shaking. The woman smiles.
My cup is empty. I pick up my book again
then put it down. We could lose our licence,
our best people could leave. The woman leans
across the table and touches the man's face.

He gazes off into the distance, nodding his head.
Demands for payment are gathering. We have
no excuses left. The man now looks at the woman.
Her smile melts into softness. The moment
between them seems to go on forever.
I pick up my empty cup. I put it down.

(ii)

It has taken it months to die and I am exhausted
from daily hope. I have no energy left for it.
Each week I wanted something less for myself –
just one month of my three-months unpaid salary,
just my accumulated expenses, just enough

to cover this train fare.
The sky is blue above a low bruising of cloud.
The small houses seem unashamed
of their littered back gardens.
Beyond the houses, the brown fields go on forever.

The Crash

Everyone wants to be paid
but we have no money.
They call me. What can I say?
I see the wedge cut out of the trunk
as I stand in the tree's shadow.
It is tilting towards me.
I hear its pain, can feel
the snap and rip of its fibers
before they explode.

We have let the staff go.
They are angry.
We have not paid ourselves
in four months.
Everyone has battened down
in this financial storm.
We cannot close any deals:
everything we do
is rain falling on sand.

I park the car, watch a cat
slink between a white wall
and a fence. The day
is bouncing in its cot
and wants to be brought
downstairs. I take the elevator up.
My desk phone is already screaming
across the empty office
when I open the door.

The Escape of Mary Bryant

Mary Bryant was one of the first convicts to escape from Botany Bay. She was eventually to win a Royal Pardon

Behind them was all that was cruel.
About them now, the sea was the same.
They had not expected it to go on forever,
to be so far from another shore. It raged,
it spat their small boat from one wave
to the next. It snatched away their last
reserves of food. There was no sky.
Ten days. They were wet to the soul.

One man, exhausted, slipped over the edge
like he was getting into bed. He just
closed his eyes, wrapped a blanket
of water over his head. They had nothing left.
She'd seen men flogged to death. This
was the same. But she was a mother,
her child a wet rag in her arms. Her voice
became the one fixed point in their world.

Her will became their will. She screamed
at them. Sure. And they pulled again
at the oars as she held the tiller steady.
One thousand miles to the Barrier Reef.
Then two thousand more. Impossible.
Yet they landed, flung themselves onto land
and held on as it bucked to a standstill.
And she wept.

At the Border

If asked if I have anything to declare,
I will not mention this poem
I carry in my mind. It is unfinished,
half-formed. It could turn into anything.
That potential is dangerous. What country
could feel safe? You're expected to know
what you carry with you.
Did you pack this poem yourself?
Does it contain any illegal utterances?
Are you under the influence
of any banned poet? No, I will pretend
that I am a novelist and keep
my story straight, a linear narrative
without metaphor or alliteration.
But what if they scan me? They now have
dogs trained to sniff out a rhyme;
observers who watch for the tell-tale sign
of fingers nervously counting iambs,
like loose change, in the pocket.
I begin to wish I'd kept my ideas
from myself until after the check-point.
Now I'm risking it all for something
that will probably be nothing.
I will be prosecuted, shamed, branded
as *Poet* for the rest of my days.

Her Car

Her car had got old, out of breath on the hill,
its body dressed in the old lines,
its chic now frumpy. When it waits
in the car park it grows tired
and can be difficult to rouse.
It has been known to suddenly
fall asleep at zebra crossings.
The dreams that cross its windscreen
are no longer of snowcapped mountains,
woodlands. Recently, it has got lost
on drives it has done all its life.
It has gone to sleep with its boot open.
Her friends have been telling her
that she should put it in a garage,
perhaps a small country one
where less would be demanded, away
from the hectic stop-start of urban journeys.
Slow lanes and soft sunsets, they tell her,
reading from the brochures.
But she is stubborn, knows
she can coax a few more miles yet
from the old girl.

She Longs for Smallness

She longs for smallness and simplicity –
a plate, a piece of bread, cheese.
She would give up the set table, the napkins,
the arrogant gleam of silverware.
There is no need for grandeur
when she has the sky.
She would cast off her silks, her brocade jacket,
her mantle of privilege. Unbleached
cotton becomes her. Her body
is its own cover. She would let down
her hair to the wind, let its braids
unfurl and lift like the hands of a child into rain.
She would let go her pain,
loosen the life she has tightened into,
let go that notion of herself
with handbags and heels. She would give up
the adulation of peers, the yes men, men.
She would live in a small house
near a harbor
and watch the boats climb the wall of the sea,
growing smaller and smaller until gone.
She would go, become one
with the sea and the sky,
leave everyone's mind, be unknown,
just a thought she holds of herself and
could easily forget.

Pluviophile

It's a sudden downpour,
the kind
that switches off the sky,
invades the ears, the eyes,
spills over itself
into the street.
All who were out on the town
now wedged
into shelter: dripping in doorways,
backs to the trunks of trees,
steaming up
phone boxes. She steps out
perhaps from an alley or from
over the bridge.
All we know is, she's here
in the limp light of a shop, standing
with her arms out,
a cruciform waterfall,
her face thrown back, eyes closed,
hair slicked
to head and neck, her clothes
darkening, fastening –
a second skin –
to her breasts, her belly, her thighs.
Her form becomes fluid, a river muscling,
all current and torque,
her body melting,
in and out of shape.
Soon she'll give way
to the storm, soon she'll be gone.

Headland

Yesterday, I watched you high on the headland,
light catching the red speck of your hair
for a moment, then going out. You had climbed
as I sat with our boys on the strand,
taking your own storm cloud into the sky.

The sea was a roar. You stood up there on the edge
of everything. The boys grew anxious. My voice
was too small to travel. The wind ambushed
even what was said amongst ourselves on the beach,
snatching my words of comfort, casting them aside.
I thought I saw the lift of your hair once more
as you shrank back from the face of the wind.

This morning a small plane unzipped the sea
from the sky, as we packed what was left of our holiday
and ourselves into the car for the long journey back.
Now we are travelling through darkness,
our car following its own lights home.

Visitation

The year after she died
she came to the door and called.
He answered

as if no time had gone by.
He let her step in.
She was pale as the moon

on a watery night, smelt
of wet leaves and grass. The day
wouldn't stay in the room.

Her voice when she spoke,
not more than a whisper
of wind through the door jam,

her eyes were dark in her head,
stars gone cold.
He stood with all of his hurt,

just stared at her face.
If he could, he'd have touched her,
held her hard to his chest.

But already the form that she had
was dimming, losing its place.
In the end she just smiled

then dissolved on the air
to his own slow implosion
of heart. But then light

came in at the window
that had not been there before.
And the day came back.

On This Dark Night

What small uncertainty triggered you afraid?
That dark stairwell that never was a thought,
possessed now with something close to dread
and nothing to tell what brought this all about.

It's as if the shadows are woven in a braid
of darker stuff just there, as if it's wrought
of something that was flesh but now, instead
of substance, an essence casting doubt

on all that's solid, safe. Now the dead
are finding a way back to hand, to mouth –
whisper, touch. Regardless of your creed
don't unwrap the mirror from its cloth.

Ah, Death

You are sure that you will know him
when you see him. But you will not.
He is not strong and tall. He is not

a warrior. He has no weapons, no voice.
It does not matter how you come
upon him, be it bomb, bullet, accident,

or sleep. See, he is just an old man sitting,
wrapped in a blanket, offering you a place
at the fire. He has not come for you.

You have come to him because it is time
to sit and gaze up at the stars, leaving
all that sits at your back behind you,

leaving everything that has a name
to its name. There is nothing more
you can say, nothing you can do.

Winter will not chill you, summer will
no longer put its warm hand on your back:
for even as we stand, we fall; even as we

welcome the morning, the afternoon
conspires against us. This is how
it happens. And the world moves on.

This Thing Called Love

For Jamal Iqbal

You try to strip it down
to its one essential – language
fighting hand-to-hand
trying to land the thing flat
on its back, defined,
laid-out, clear, laid to rest.

But that's not how it works.
The pure clean arc of the story
you hold in your head
is party-time, demonstration.

The give and take of love
doesn't balance like that –
the sweeping leg misses, the counter
throw is countered. There are points
to be made and submissions.
It's all in the grip-fighting.

The Fallen

1 Visit

I found her soft-landed, crouched in the garden,
gilded in the thrown shape of the window.
Her eyes were feral, her tufted hair startled with light.
When she uncurled upwards it was as fluent as language,
a warning I stepped back from.

Her nakedness was a sudden silence.
She snarled, came close, her breasts sharp.
I was lost in the long moment of her gaze.
Her tongue was a small bird in the nest of her mouth.
She stepped into the house.

Feathers were bunched from her shoulder blades
to the small of her back. She passed through my rooms
singing. I could have stared all night, my heart dancing.
But she left as easily as she came, massive wings erupting,
lifting her into the dark.

2 Dust

She's back again, a benediction. My world blooms,
my heart skitters. Beside her I feel impure, fractured.
Her small arms encompass me. She asks
Why did love come now after its long silence?
I am possessed by her old habit of adoration.

Is this what my banishment is for –
to stand at this window looking in on a meal
yet never break bread. Here is the wine of my dream:
to be corporal, to feel. The price of immortality, she tells me
is perfection, and who would want that?
She believes she will gain humanity by being with me.

She who had never known sex is urgent with need,
willing to give of herself, to be taken again and again.
Pain has its compensations. *I want to be ugly,* she says.
I want that one day it will be over,
that dust will be dust and will settle.

Achille Island

for Marie

We took sun-bleached roads to Achille –
a day to get there, a week packed on our backs,
the whole country to cross.

Few cars stopped for us.
We chased our shadows down until
we overtook them, riding in a farmer's car,
to pitch our tent
amongst the melted shapes of evening.

That night it rained and never stopped.
When we awoke we found the beach
crouched beneath a weight of sky;
watched the mountains ease from skirts of mist
to touch the grey skin of the sea.

We paid no homage to elemental gods.
We were our own beginnings,
running the shore's green-crisped edge.
Within the flappings of our tent we opened up
the future from crumpled sleeping bags.

The sun burst forth the day we packed,
stared us down, amazed to see us laugh,
as we walked the same roads back.

Kites

Hanging from the sky
at the tail-end of a Wexford summer:
two boys flying kites.

The dipped field spins the clouds
and the cows waiting
to be milked bow their shoulders

at the dairy door, swim
into the calf's sad glance.
Fighting the long line to land,

we too could be kites
above the spoon of the meadow,
full of the moment's gift –

the slow unbuttoning of a mind
unburdened in this naked land.
Soon the milk

of this sky will be pailed
into evening. But for this while
our ribbons dance.

By the Hawthorn Hedge

That morning when I came down to the door flung back
and the wind lifting the sleeves of my coat, hung in the hall,

a chill entered me. And though I piled on the turf
till my shins burned, it would not go.

I watched then, as my wife eased herself through the house,
her hair, red as my own, tumbling when she stooped

to lift the baby to suckle at her breast. It would not take much.
The shock of its black hair silken beneath her fingers.

Back in the cot I'd made out of wood, carved with a knife,
it would stare cold into my eyes.

It turned old in a matter of weeks.
I would not pick it up.

We buried it by the hawthorn hedge. *Let its own come*
I said, *and take it back*, remembering the dried sticks

of its legs, the body pale as the sheet on which it lay
and my wife, open mouthed, hammering fists against her thighs.

Faceless

I call in on Margaret with my sister.
Sure, I knew your mother well.
Margaret's eighty if she is a day.

When she was a young one, working
in that shop above in town,
I'd call in on her for a chat.

But them days, they'd be
watching you, you know,
so you wouldn't stop for long.

There's no chatting nowadays at all.
Them days you knew everyone.
The Mourn Mountains are a grey haze

at the bottom of her rain-soft garden.
We slowly sip our tea, our Irish welcome.
She shows us her new armchair.

It's sure to see me out. Her cat
has claimed the old one,
scratch marks already laddering the legs.

Going home my sister tells me
She's terrified of being found dead
in that house by herself. You know,

a cat will eat the face of you
if it finds you dead, the door locked.
I'm a stranger to the ways of cats

but I like the idea of this,
if not the act –
to arrive faceless at that last gate.

Trouble with Women

I never should have taken her to the mall.
It was not something she was used to –
being ripped out of the story I was writing
and squeezed into a seat on the metro.
People need to believe in you, I tell her.
Well you are the one who dressed me
in these ankle socks, she sneers - not the kind
of attitude I expect from one of my characters
so I ignore her a while. But she begins to look,
I mean LOOK, at the boys who look at me and I
have to distract her. *You think I'm a virgin,*
she says, *an innocent. If you want to dress*
differently.. She walks me into a clothes shop,
where I find myself engrossed in lingerie,
thinking about cup size, the discomfort
of a g-string. I'm escorted out of the shop
by her. She's decided to eat. In the restaurant,
she sits quietly, demure, a young lady at last.
I'm about to order a beetroot salad with feta
when she interrupts with *a burger and fries*
even calls after the waiter, *Make it large, make*
it quick. I now have her back on the page but
my story's goes all out of whack when she strips
off her socks, changes into something I'd seen float
from a hanger – a gauzy whisper of silk. As I write,
there's a knock on her door. I turn down the light.

Ladywood 1977

It was a bus ride, sometimes two,
jerking through traffic, to the city centre stop.
You could see the stop from the pedestrian bridge
out of the Bullring Centre
but could seldom find your way down to it
through the shops and exit signs.
We bargained for cheese and grapes in the market,
and, if we could afford it, a bottle of red.
The journey home was always heavier.
Not just because of the bags that lengthened our arms,
but because of the quality of light – the day tipping
into evening, the shops greying into terraces,
and always hoping that the rain that glimmered
on the misted window would ease
as we drove down Hagley Road to our stop.
Then the walk to that mid-terrace house
where a bedroom had been partitioned
into our 'flat'; the house with the hooker
on the ground floor and the man that beat his wife
on the second, we watching sails improbably float
between the gables opposite – Edgbaston Reservoir –
as we tried to make a go of it in between.

The Wide Ocean of the Sky

For my wife, Marie, on the occasion of her 60th birthday

What a challenge you are in your white
gi, your low centre of gravity, your technique,
turning into me, taking me over.

What a possibility. Such changes – me stepping up
to your game. Come into my dark coat.
See how it locks out the cold.

What a furnace of hair. Impossible not to be
consumed by the thought of it
here in the winter of my breath-spumed bedroom.

This is what I give to you: one room
disguised as a flat, the worst part of town,
strange accents, black men, rain chucking it,

and gifts which I hid – a porcelain rose in a drawer,
costume jewelry blinking light on window ledges,
a gilded pen in the spine of a book.

Your sanity worries you. You see sails floating
between the gables opposite. Sky boats. Strangeness.
This city is a weight on your mind. I gave you this too.

Now this walk in the wet, the houses crowding,
the streets all glint and edge, and now
on a turn of steps, Birmingham Reservoir, widening out

like a gasp, drinking in all the light of the sky.
A place saved up until today, until this circle
back to our flat; a place of escape.

Here are the sail boats traversing the cloudy sky
and here is the sun coming, bursting with its shout.
Listen, small lappings too at our feet.

Here we are again in the Fire Salvage Shop
on Edgbaston Road looking for a fix,
looking for stories we will tell about ourselves.

You have your hair cropped tight, you wear smart
business suits. You go to sit at a desk. Can you believe
the people we've become? Money in the bank.

There's no need to be told where we came from.
We're ourselves. We've doubled each other.
We are our own green island.

> We eat where yellow mornings splash
> the glazed pine floor;
> where a dresser sits smug against a wall.
> We eat at a bench table
> where we can set our elbows down
> to look across to see each other smile.
>
> The lounge has one louvered wall of pine,
> one we've shelved with books. Sometimes
> I set a cine projector up so we can watch ourselves
> flicker into life – squared energy and motion –
> until the reel slaps out and into circles;
> until the square fills up with light.

Now you are a baby whale in a tent of a dress.
You are my own fat moon, pulling the tide in,
waiting for your waters to break.

Look how joined-up we are:
father, mother, son – that timeless circle –
like we've just found out that we are gods.

We have more tents to create now in the living room,
and tunnels: sheets and pegs and chairs,
a whole new universe to crawl through.

This is the first time I think of you as old –
giving away fifteen years to this bigger woman.
Your old confidence is in hiding; it will not come out.

I fret that you'll get hurt. All I can do is watch.
You're outmatched in strength but you spin,
a left-handed *makakomi*, an oldie,

a throw from the early days, here like
the slamming of a door through its arc. She's flat
on her back and you are the Essex women's champion.

You have a way on the phone to open village hall doors;
get free passes to fun parks – the children's rock choir tour
starting its life in our living room.

And now we're on tour: a bus full of noise.
We invade the village hall's kitchen with boxes of food,
we roll out sleeping bags, small fields of evening.

How angelic they look, those tear-aways, that
squabbling swarm, now swaying the audience, beating
the drum. How I love watching you watching them.

The day dulls, the car grows small about us.
You are not well, you are clouded, weary. You are dark.
You darken the car. The road rushes under us.

You are tracking your own journey, shakily reeling
back through images. That furious pull into the self –
your mother who has wandered back into her youth,

a son who has stood for an hour and a half on one foot,
terrified of taking a step. Houses pass, whipping by
on their grass carpets, then terraces like buses.

Our son sees newborns packed on the floor
and not a safe inch on which he might put
down his weight, till he can't stay up, gone in his mind,

goes down. Murderer. Dooming himself to hell. You hold
it together. Daughter. Mother. We are headed for home.
It is time, I feel, for you to be astonished

by something you might have wished for: a small cup
of calm; a moment of nothing but standing
under the quiet dark of a sleeping sky.

You are stalled by the heat – Dubai Airport. I have come
to pick you up. *A Bedouin tent,* I tell you, *two camels parked
at the side.* But I drive you to a villa; Arab-styled, it towers

off-white against a tatter of sky. We stand
in the double story living space – so much of it, so
cool and quiet. Ours. *Can we afford this? The bank thinks we can.*

You admire the furniture - don't scold me for buying it
without you - the double-back staircase, the sort you might grace
in a dream. You give me your hand. I take you to bed.

Now you're seven hours away in rain.
I'm in the ruin of our dream. I phone to hold to your voice.
You should come home, you say, but nothing seems possible.

After the violent storm, wreckage floats to the top.
We gather what we can of our financial flotsam,
back in Dubai, starting over: this rented apartment,

the two of us smoothing clean sheets across a bed.
What else do we need but the surprise of each other?
We know about wealth: it grows on the trees

> I want to rise again
> in curtained calm,
> to lightly step a sleepy road,
> to meet the sun on the hill waking,
> watch the rooks shake out the trees,
> have a place where I can slow,
> forget our cash flow's steady erosion,
> the spreadsheet's numbers red insisting,
> the Company's Act, the regulations,
> those legal clauses clogging vision,
> being the last car in the parking lot,
> all the lies I tell my heart
> to keep it going.
>
> I want to rise to softer cares
> with toast and tea and breakfast table,
> you in your smiling chair,
> the garden green against the gable,
> the door contented with its swing,
> letting out or in or standing,
> a mountain yawning in its bed,
> a postman humming.

like the years that have fluttered off, one at a time,
you hardly notice them going till they rustle behind you.
You turn and then turn back from their gold,

for as the Irish should have said *milsigh birth bother* and
surely still half of that double journey ahead.
What an adventure we shall make of it. What a quest.

The same prize each day: you with your smiling voice.
Who needs a destination, a palace, a kingdom?
We have the road. We have the wide ocean of the sky.

**milsigh birth bother – two sweeten the road.*